FIRST dictionary

make believe ideas

a b c d e f g h i j k l m n o p q r s t u v w x y z

Aa

ambulance

An **ambulance** is a special van that takes people to hospital when they are hurt or sick.

aeroplane

An **aeroplane** is a flying machine with wings that carries people and things.

angry

If you are **angry**, you feel very upset and annoyed.

animal

An **animal** is a living thing that moves around. A plant is not an animal. Cats, chickens, spiders and goldfish are all animals.

alphabet

An **alphabet** is a collection of letters used in writing, arranged in a special order.

apple

An **apple** is a round juicy fruit that grows on a tree. Its skin can be green, red or yellow.

Bb

ball

A **ball** is a round object used in games. You can throw, hit, catch, roll or kick a ball.

bat

A **bat** is a piece of wood that is used to hit a ball in a game.

ball

bat

banana

A **banana** is a long fruit with a thick, yellow skin.

basket

A **basket** is a container used to store or carry things.

bee

A **bee** is an insect with wings. Bees make honey.

wing

beetle

A **beetle** is an insect that has hard, shiny wing covers.

bed

A **bed** is something you lie down and sleep on.

bicycle

A **bicycle** is a machine you ride. It has two wheels and pedals.

bird

A **bird** is an animal with wings, feathers and a beak. Most birds can fly.

body

The **body** of a person or an animal is every part of them.

bowl

A **bowl** is a deep dish that holds food like soup, breakfast cereal or fruit.

bread

Bread is a food mad with flour. It is baked in an oven.

box

A **box** is used to keep things in. Most boxes are made of plastic or cardboard.

broccoli

Broccoli is a green vegetable.

book

A **book** is made up of lots of pages held together inside a cover.

boy

A **boy** is a child who will grow up to be a man.

brush

A **brush** has lots of stiff hairs or wires and usually has a handle.

bottle

A **bottle** holds liquid. It is usually made of glass or plastic.

bucket

A **bucket** is used to carry things like liquids or sand.

bulldozer

A **bulldozer** is a big machine with a shovel that pushes rocks out of the way.

shovel

cake

A **cake** is a sweet food. It is made by mixing butter, sugar, eggs and flour and baking it in an oven.

bus

A **bus** is a long vehicle with seats inside to carry people around.

button

A **button** is a small object that fastens clothes together.

butterfly

A **butterfly** is an insect that has large, colourful wings.

car

A **car** is a machine with four wheels and an engine that we use to get from one place to another.

a b **c** d e f g h i j k l m n o p q r s t u v w x y z

carrot

A **carrot** is a long, orange vegetable that grows under the ground.

cat

A **cat** is an animal with soft fur, sharp claws and a long tail. People keep small cats as pets.

catch

When you **catch** something, you take hold of it while it is moving.

caterpillar

A **caterpillar** looks like a worm with legs. It turns into a butterfly or a moth.

chair

back

A **chair** is a seat with four legs and a back.

leg

cheese

Cheese is a food made from milk.

child

A **child** is a young boy or girl. When there is more than one child, they are called children.

chocolate

Chocolate is a sweet food made from cocoa beans.

clock

A **clock** is a machine that shows you what time it is.

clown

A **clown** is someone who says and does funny things to make people laugh.

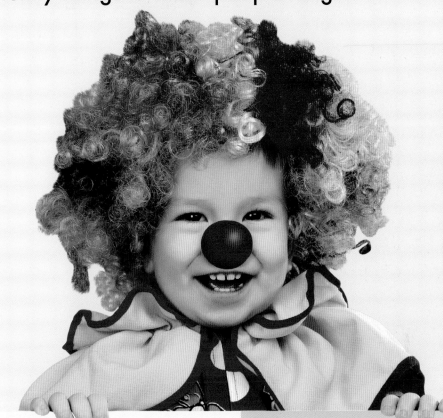

clothes

Clothes are the things that people wear, such as shirts, trousers and dresses.

colour

Red, blue and yellow are **colours**. By mixing them together, you get other colours.

computer

A **computer** is a machine that stores information and helps people to work.

comb

A **comb** is a piece of plastic or metal that has lots of thin teeth. You use a comb to fix your hair.

a b c d e f g h i j k l m n o p q r s t u v w x y z

7

A B C D E F G H I J K L M N O P Q R S T U V W X Y Z

cow

A **cow** is a large female farm animal that produces milk. The male animal is called a bull and the baby is a calf.

crown

A **crown** is a kind of hat, usually worn by kings and queens. It is often made of gold or silver.

cry

When you **cry**, tears fall from your eyes.

cucumber

A **cucumber** is a long, green vegetable.

crawl

When you **crawl**, you move around on your hands and knees.

cup

A **cup** is a small, round container with a handle. You drink from a cup.

handle

crocodile

A **crocodile** is an animal with sharp teeth, short legs and a long tail.

tail

8 tooth

leg

Ee

elephant

An **elephant** is a large, grey animal that has tusks, big ears and a long nose called a trunk.

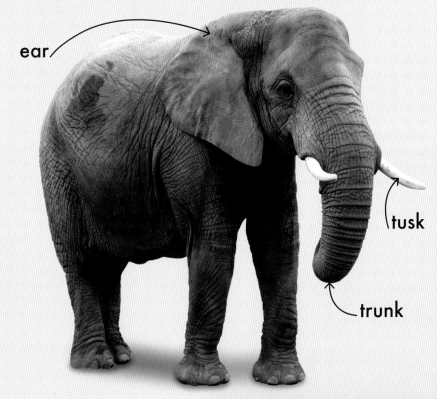

ear

tusk

trunk

eagle

An **eagle** is a large bird with big wings, a curved beak and sharp claws.

ear

Your **ears** are on each side of your head. You hear with your ears.

envelope

An **envelope** is a paper cover to put letters or cards inside.

eye

Your **eyes** are on your face. You see with your eyes.

egg

Many animals, such as birds, lizards and some fish live inside **eggs** until they are big enough to hatch out.

exercise

When you **exercise**, you move your body to keep fit.

Dd

doctor

A **doctor** takes care of people who are sick or hurt and helps them to get better.

dice

Dice are small cubes that have a different number of spots on each side.

dinosaur

Dinosaurs were animals that lived on Earth millions of years ago.

dish

A **dish** is a bowl for serving food.

dog

A **dog** is an animal that barks. Dogs are often kept as pets.

donkey

A **donkey** is a furry animal that looks like a small horse with long ears.

ear

a b c d e f g h i j k l m n o p q r s t u v w x y z

Ff

face

Your **face** is the front part of your head. Your eyes, nose and mouth are all part of your face.

family

Your **family** is the group of people that are closest to you. Your mum, dad, brothers and sisters are all part of your family.

farm

A **farm** is a place where farmers grow food and raise animals.

feather

Birds have **feathers** on their bodies to keep them warm and dry. Feathers also help birds fly.

feather

finger

Your **fingers** are part of your hand. Each hand has four fingers and a thumb.

fire

A **fire** is the hot, bright flames and smoke made when something is burning.

fire engine

A **fire engine** is a vehicle with a ladder and a water hose. Firefighters use fire engines to drive to fires and put them out.

flower

A **flower** is part of a plant. Many flowers smell nice and are bright colours.

food

Food is what you eat to keep you strong and healthy.

frog

A **frog** is a small animal that lives in damp places.

fish

A **fish** is an animal that lives in water. Fish have fins to swim and gills to "breathe" under water.

gills

fin

fork

A **fork** has sharp prongs and a handle. You use a small fork for eating and a big fork for digging in the garden.

fruit

A **fruit** is the part of a plant that holds the seeds. Lots of fruits, such as apples and grapes, are juicy and good to eat.

Gg

game

A **game** is what you play for fun. Bat and ball is a game.

gate

A **gate** is a kind of door in a wall, fence or hedge.

giraffe

A **giraffe** is a tall animal with long legs and a very long neck.

neck

legs

goat

A **goat** is an animal with long hair and horns on its head.

grape

A **grape** is a small purple or green fruit that grows in bunches. Grapes are used to make wine.

girl

A **girl** is a child who will grow up to be a woman.

grow

When somebody or something **grows**, it gets bigger.

a b c d e f **g** h i j k l m n o p q r s t u v w x y z

Hh

helicopter

A **helicopter** is a flying machine with blades that spin instead of wings. The blades allow it to lift up straight from the ground and hover.

blade

half

A **half** is one of two pieces that are equal in size.

hammer

A **hammer** is a tool you can use to hit nails into wood.

hop

You **hop** when you jump up and down on one leg.

house

A **house** is a building where people eat, sleep and live. Houses have roofs, walls, doors and windows to keep the people inside warm and dry.

head

Your **head** is the part of your body that is above your neck.

horse

A **horse** is a big animal with hooves. People ride horses and use them to pull heavy loads.

Ii

ice

Ice is made when water freezes. It is very cold and hard.

ice cream

Ice cream is a sweet, creamy, frozen food.

idea

An **idea** is a thought you have about something.

insects

An **insect** is a small animal with six legs. Many insects have wings. Ants, beetles, butterflies and bees are all insects.

Jj

jar

Jars are usually made of glass. They close tightly and keep foods, like jam, fresh.

jewel

A **jewel** is a beautiful, sparkling stone. Some jewels, like diamonds, cost a lot of money.

A B C D E F G H I J K L M N O P Q R S T U V W X Y Z

jigsaw puzzle

A **jigsaw puzzle** is made from lots of pieces that fit together to make a picture.

Kk

kid

A **kid** is the name for a baby goat. Children can also be called kids.

juice

Juice is the liquid that comes out of a fruit when you squeeze it.

key

A **key** is a specially shaped piece of metal that is used to lock or unlock a door.

king

A **king** is a man who is born to rule a country.

jump

When you **jump**, you push both feet off the ground and move suddenly up into the air.

kick

When you **kick** something, you hit it with your foot.

knife

A **knife** is a tool used for cutting. Most knives have a handle and a long, sharp, metal blade.

16

Ll

ladder

You use a **ladder** to climb up high. Ladders are made of metal or wood.

lamp

A **lamp** gives you light. You can move a lamp around and switch it on and off.

leaf

A **leaf** is one of the flat, green parts of a plant or tree.

letter

A **letter** is a sign you use to write words. A, m and z are all letters. A letter is also what you can write to a friend or relative.

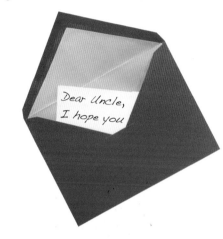

Dear Uncle,
I hope you

lion

A **lion** is a big, wild cat. Lions live in Africa and India.

lamb

A **lamb** is a young sheep that is still with its mother.

lamb

lemon

A **lemon** is a juicy, yellow fruit with a sour taste.

a
b
c
d
e
f
g
h
i
j
k
l
m
n
o
p
q
r
s
t
u
v
w
x
y
z

Mm

mask

A **mask** is something that you wear to cover your face. People wear masks to change the way they look.

man

A **man** is a grown-up male person.

medicine

You take **medicine** when you are sick in order to make you well again.

milk

Milk is a white liquid that mother animals make to feed their babies. Many people drink cows' milk.

map

A **map** is a drawing that shows you where places are so you can find your way around.

mirror

A **mirror** is a sheet c special glass that you can see yourself in.

money

Money is the bills and coins that you use to buy things.

mountain

A **mountain** is a very tall piece of land or rock.

moon

The **moon** shines in the sky at night. It is a big ball of rock that moves slowly around the Earth about once a month.

mouse

A **mouse** is a small, furry animal with a long tail. Mice have sharp front teeth for gnawing food.

mushroom

A **mushroom** is a living thing that looks like a little umbrella. You can eat some mushrooms.

mug

A **mug** is a large, straight cup with a handle. You drink hot drinks from a mug.

music

Music is the sound that people make when they sing or play instruments.

motorbike

A **motorbike** is a vehicle with two wheels and an engine.

a b c d e f g h i j k l **m** n o p q r s t u v w x y z

net

A **net** is made from pieces of string or thread tied together with holes in between. Nets are used for catching fish and also in games such as tennis and football.

ball

net

needle

A **needle** is a thin, smooth piece of metal used for sewing. It is sharp at one end and has a hole for thread at the other.

needle

thread

nose

Your **nose** is part of your face. You use it for breathing and smelling.

nurse

A **nurse** is a person who takes care of people who are sick or hurt. Nurses often work in hospitals.

nest

A **nest** is the home that animals like birds and mice make for their babies.

20

number

A **number** tells you how many you have of something. 3 and 100 are numbers.

Oo

opposite

An **opposite** is completely different. The opposite of full is empty.

full

empty

orange

An **orange** is a round, juicy fruit with orange-coloured peel.

oven

An **oven** is the compartment in a cooker where you roast or bake food.

owl

An **owl** is a bird that hunts for small animals at night. It has big eyes to help it see in the dark.

Pp

paint

Paint is a liquid that you put on to things to change the colour.

paper

Paper is a very thin material used for drawing and writing.

parrot

A **parrot** is a bird with brightly coloured feathers and a sharp, curved beak. Some parrots can talk.

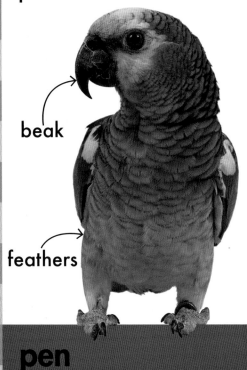

beak

feathers

penguin

Penguins are seabirds with black-and-white feathers that mostly live on cold, rocky coastlines. Penguins cannot fly but use their wings as flippers to swim.

flipper

pen

You use a **pen** to write or draw in ink.

pencil

A **pencil** is a long, thin stick of wood with black or coloured lead in the middle. Pencils are used for writing and drawing.

22

pet

A **pet** is a tame animal that you take care of in your home. Dogs, cats and hamsters are often kept as pets.

pig

A **pig** is an animal with a fat body, short legs and a curly tail.

pirate

A **pirate** is a sailor who attacks and robs other sailors at sea.

plate

A **plate** is a flat dish that you put food on.

pumpkin

A **pumpkin** is a large fruit with orange skin.

play

When you **play**, you have fun with your friends and join in games. Children and baby animals love to play with toys.

puppet

A **puppet** is a toy figure. You move a puppet by pulling strings or by putting your hand inside it.

plant

A **plant** is a living thing that grows in soil or water. Trees, flowers and grass are all plants.

present

A **present** is something special that you give to someone to make them happy.

Qq

queen

A **queen** is a woman who is born to rule a country. A king's wife is also called a queen.

question

A **question** is what you ask when you want to know something.

Rr

read

When you **read**, you understand words that are written down.

rabbit

A **rabbit** is a small, furry animal with long ears and a fluffy tail.

ear

rain

Rain is lots of little drops of water that fall from the clouds.

rainbow

A **rainbow** is an arch of bright colours that you see when the sun shines through rain.

rhinoceros

A **rhinoceros** is a big animal with tough, leathery skin and horns on its head.

robot

A **robot** is a machine that can do some of the jobs that people do.

Ss

sandwich

A **sandwich** is made of two slices of bread with a filling, such as cheese or ham, between them.

scissors

A pair of **scissors** is a tool used to cut paper or cloth. Scissors have two sharp blades and two handles.

rocket

A **rocket** is the part of a spacecraft that pushes it high into space.

saucepan

A **saucepan** is a deep, metal cooking pot with a handle and usually a lid.

shape

The **shape** of something is its outline or the way it looks on the outside.

ruler

A **ruler** is a long, flat tool used for drawing lines and measuring length.

saw

A **saw** is a tool with sharp, metal teeth for cutting through wood.

25

shark

A **shark** is a big fish. Some sharks have very sharp teeth and can attack people.

snake

A **snake** has a long body and no legs. Its skin is made of scales.

sheep

A **sheep** is an animal with a thick, woolly coat. Male sheep are called rams, females are called ewes and babies are called lambs.

shoe

You wear **shoes** on your feet to protect them.

snowman

A **snowman** is made out of snow and shaped like a person.

sleep

When you **sleep**, you close your eyes and rest.

shell

A **shell** is a hard covering around something. Shellfish and nuts have shells.

smile

A **smile** is when the corners of your mouth turn up. You smile when you feel happy.

sock

You wear **socks** on your feet to keep them warm.

spade

A **spade** is a tool used to dig holes in the ground. It has a long handle and a flat, metal end.

strawberry

A **strawberry** is a soft, sweet, red fruit with seeds on it.

spider

A **spider** is an animal with eight legs. Spiders spin webs to catch insects for food.

leg

squirrel

A **squirrel** is a small, furry animal that lives in trees. It has a bushy tail and eats nuts.

sun

The **Sun** shines in the sky and gives the Earth light and heat. It is a star and the Earth moves around it.

star

A **star** is a small, bright light in the sky. You can see stars on a clear, dark night. A star is also a shape with five or more points.

swan

A **swan** is a large bird with a long neck. It lives on rivers and lakes.

spoon

A **spoon** has a long handle and a round part at one end. You use a spoon to eat foods like soup and cereal.

starfish

A **starfish** is an animal with five arms that lives in the ocean. It is shaped like a star.

a b c d e f g h i j k l m n o p q r s t u v w x y z

A B C D E F G H I J K L M N O P Q R S T U V W X Y Z

Tt

table

A **table** is a piece of furniture with legs and a flat top. You can eat at a table.

tail

An animal's **tail** grows at the end of its body. It helps the animal to balance.

tail

telephone

A **telephone** is a machine you use to talk to someone in another place.

tent

A **tent** is a shelter made out of a piece of cloth stretched over metal poles. You use a tent for camping.

thermometer

You use a **thermometer** to find out how hot or cold something is.

tiger

A **tiger** is a big, wild cat with orange-and-black striped fur. Wild tigers are rare, but some still live in India and China.

tomato

A **tomato** is a soft, red, round fruit that you often eat in salads.

towel

A **towel** is a piece of soft, thick cloth that you use to dry yourself.

tree

A **tree** is a tall plant with leaves, branches and a thick stem of wood called a trunk.

tool

A **tool** is something you hold in your hands to help you do things. Spanners, saws and hammers are all tools.

toy

A **toy** is something a child plays with. Dolls, kites, teddy bears and train sets are all toys.

truck

A **truck** is a strong vehicle that takes things from one place to another.

toothbrush

You use a **toothbrush** and toothpaste to keep your teeth clean.

tractor

A **tractor** is a farm vehicle with big back wheels to pull things.

wheel

29

a b c d e f g h i j k l m n o p q r s t u v w x y z

A
B
C
D
E
F
G
H
I
J
K
L
M
N
O
P
Q
R
S
T
U
V
W
X
Y
Z

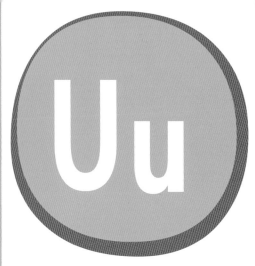

Uu

umbrella

An **umbrella** keeps you dry when it rains.

uniform

Some people wear a **uniform** to show what job they do or which school they go to.

Vv

vacuum cleaner

A **vacuum cleaner** is a machine that sucks up dust and dirt.

vase

A **vase** is a kind of container you can use to hold cut flowers in water.

vegetable

A **vegetable** is a plant that can be eaten raw or cooked. Carrots, cabbages and onions are all vegetables.

violin

A **violin** is a musical instrument made of wood. You play it using a bow.

bow

violin

Ww

wheel

Wheels are round and they can turn. Bicycles, cars and trains all have wheels so that they can move.

watch

A **watch** is a small clock that you can wear on your wrist. It tells you what time it is.

Xx

X-ray

An **X-ray** is a picture that lets a doctor see inside your body.

water

Water is a clear liquid found in rivers, lakes and oceans. Water also comes out of taps.

woman

A **woman** is a grown-up female person.

xylophone

A **xylophone** is a musical instrument with a row of wooden bars.

a b c d e f g h i j k l m n o p q r s t u v w x y z

yogurt

Yogurt is a food made from milk. It is often mixed with fruit.

yacht

A **yacht** is a boat with sails or an engine. Yachts are used for fun.

sail

yolk

The **yolk** is the middle part of an egg.

yolk

zebra

A **zebra** looks like a horse with black-and-white stripes. Zebras live in Africa.

yo-yo

A **yo-yo** is a round toy that you roll up and down on a string.

string

yawn

When you **yawn**, you open your mouth wide and breathe out noisily.

zip

A **zip** joins two pieces of material together. The zip's teeth lock together when you close it.

FIRST dictionary

Thematic pages

Wild animals

Animals are known as **wild animals** if they move around freely in the oceans, in the air or on the land.

snake

frog

eagle

crocodile

eye

tail

foot

shark

elephant

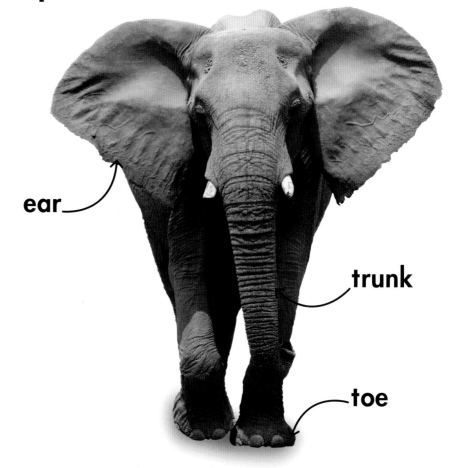

ear

trunk

toe

tiger

Farm animals

People keep **farm animals** for food such as meat or milk, and for their skin or fur.

horse

foal

cockerel

pig

goat

chick

sheep

cows

Pets

A **pet** is a tame animal, such as a dog or a hamster, that you look after, often in your home or garden.

dog

pony

mane

nose

cat

hamster

goldfish

rabbit

macaw

guinea pig

Birds

A **bird** is an animal with wings, feathers and a beak. Most birds are able to fly.

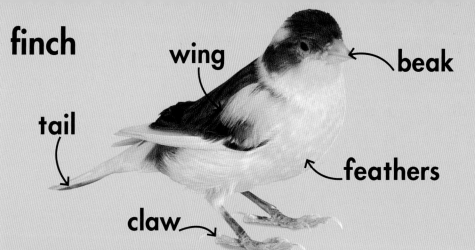

finch

wing

beak

tail

feathers

claw

owl

eagle

swan

hornbill

pigeon

ostrich

penguins

37

Insects

An **insect** is a small animal with six legs. An insect's body is divided into three parts. Some insects have wings.

bee

fly

butterflies

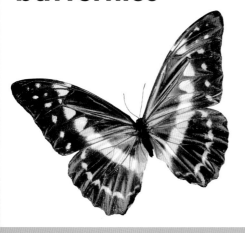

wasp

leg

ant

dragonfly

wing

grasshopper

ladybird

Food

Food is anything that you eat to help you grow and keep you healthy. Cheese, vegetables, fruit and bread are all food.

sandwich

pasta

carrots

pie

cupcake

nuts

sausages

bread

cheese

banana

Fruit

A **fruit** is the part of a plant that holds the seeds. Many fruits are juicy and delicious to eat.

grapes

watermelon

pineapple

starfruit

seed

apple

strawberry

banana

peel

peach

tomato

raspberry

Vegetables

A **vegetable** is the part of a plant that is used for food. Beans, cabbages, cauliflowers, onions, potatoes and peas are all vegetables.

leek

cabbage

pepper

onion

broccoli

peas

sweetcorn

potato

beans

cauliflower

Body

Your **body** is every part of you, from your head to your toes. The different parts of your body work together to keep you alive and healthy.

head

foot

neck

finger

thumb

back

bottom

shoulder

wrist

knuckles

elbow

face

hand

arm

chest

stomach

hips

thigh

knee

leg

shin

calf

ankle

toe

heel

43

Face

Your **face** is the front part of your head. Your eyes, nose and mouth are all parts of your face.

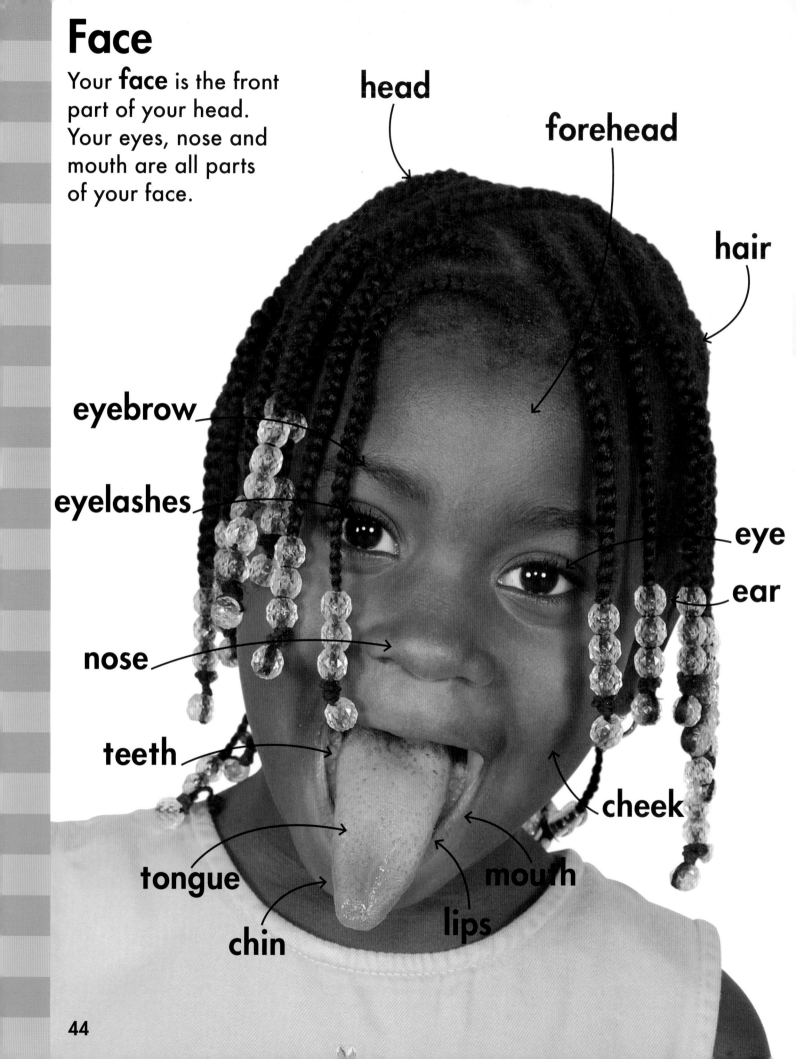

head

forehead

hair

eyebrow

eyelashes

eye

ear

nose

teeth

cheek

tongue

mouth

chin

lips

Clothes

Clothes are things that people wear. Socks, shoes, shirts, trousers and hats are all clothes.

hat

gloves

boots

underpants

shirt

shorts

pyjamas

scarf

dress

shoes

laces

Family

A **family** is a group of people who are related to each other. Most families have parents, children and grandchildren.

mother

sisters

grandfather

aunt

grandmother

boy

brothers

cousins

girl

father

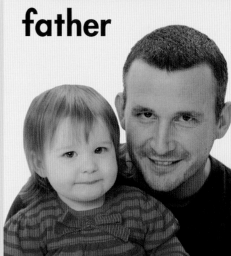

46

Garden

A **garden** is where people grow flowers and vegetables. A person's garden is usually next to his or her house.

ant

watering can

acorn

flower

stem

trowel

handle

spider

tree

trunk

frog

boots

Home

Your **home** is the place where you live. A home usually has a kitchen, a living room, a bathroom and one or more bedrooms.

sofa

table

bath

lamp

chair

fireplace

Kitchen

A **kitchen** is where food is stored and prepared. A kitchen usually contains a refrigerator, cooker, sink and cupboards.

saucepan

sieve

fork

plate

knife

spoon

spoon

rolling pin

cookie cutters

cooker

apron

Toys

A **toy** is something you play with. Dolls, teddy bears, kites, train sets and jigsaw puzzles are all toys.

tricycle

doll

jigsaw puzzle

train

wheel

balloons

ball

teddy bears

dinosaur

bat

kite

blocks

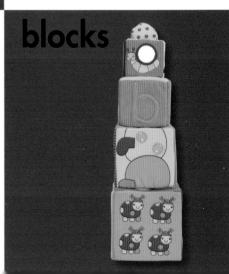

Tools

A **tool** is something you use to help you do a job. Hammers, screwdrivers, saws, drills and spanners are all tools.

drill

spanners

scissors

blade

bucket

spade

screwdrivers

watering can

hammer

pliers

trowel

tool box

School

School is the place you go to learn. At school, teachers teach children how to read, write, count and other important things.

teacher

glue

books

triangle

violin

ruler

paints

paper
pen

brushes

tambourine
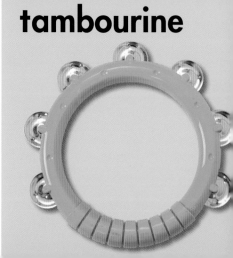

Beach

A **beach** is the strip of land on the edge of the sea. Beaches are usually covered with sand or pebbles.

bucket

deckchair

sandcastle

spade

swimsuit

windmill

starfish

arm

shell

boat

Things that go

Trucks, trains, buses and cars carry people and goods on land. Boats travel on the water and planes fly through the air.

truck

helicopter

blade

car

scooter

hot-air balloon

basket

tractor

aeroplane

ambulance

bicycle

quad bike

rocket

bus

train

boat

motorbike

bulldozer

van

wheel

dumper

fire engine

55

Doing words

Words that describe what we are doing are known as verbs. Most verbs describe actions, such as eating, drinking, reading or jumping.

hopping

skipping

rope

crouching

bathing

swinging

walking

hugging

yawning

kissing

catching

crawling

Time

Time is measured in minutes, hours, days, weeks, months and years. The time is a particular moment in the day.

Days of the week

Sunday

Monday

Tuesday

Wednesday

Thursday

Friday

Saturday

Months

January

February

March

April

May

June

July

August

September

October

November

December

Seasons

spring

summer

autumn

winter

four o'clock

quarter past four

half past four

quarter to five

57

Shapes

A **shape** is the way an object looks on the outside, or the pattern you make when you draw around it. Circles, squares and triangles are shapes.

circle

star

heart

rectangle

triangle

cheese

square

pentagon

spiral

cylinder

sphere

cube

Colours

Red, yellow and blue are **colours**. By mixing them together you can make other colours, such as green, purple and orange.

black

blue

red

yellow

green

brown

grey

orange

white

purple

pink

Opposites

When things are the **opposite** of each other, they are completely different. Tall is the opposite of short and hot is the opposite of cold.

awake

asleep

light

dark

big

hot   **cold**

little

dirty

clean

dry

baby

wet

full empty

tall

fast

hare

slow

snail

thin

fat

tortoise

old

new

open

short

shut

happy

sad

Numbers

Numbers tell you how many people or things there are. A number can be written as a word (one, two, three) or as a numeral (1, 2, 3).

1 one frog

2 two babies

6 six tractors

7 seven puppies

20 twenty cupcakes

50 fifty jelly beans

3 three kittens

4 four spanners

5 five tomatoes

8 eight flowers

9 nine ducklings

10 ten paints

100 one hundred buttons